FULL SPEED AHEAD

by Pete Birle

Full Speed Ahead
COPYRIGHT 2008
by Pete Birle

Scobre Press Corporation
2255 Calle Clara
La Jolla, CA 92037

Scobre Press books may be purchased for
educational, business or sales promotional use.
First Scobre edition published 2008.

Edited by Charlotte Graeber
Cover Art & Layout by Michael Lynch

ISBN # 1-934713-02-3

HOME RUN EDITION
This story is based on the real life of Bryson McLeod, although
some names, quotes, and details of events have been altered.

Chapter One

In the Game

Imagine that you've just received a pass at the top of the key. You shield the basketball with your body so it won't be stolen. You look at the hoop. Your grip on the ball tightens as a defender approaches. Too far out to launch a jump shot, you look down low. There's a lot happening beneath the basket. Elbows are flying as your teammates try to get position. The defense, meanwhile, is trying hard to deny them the ball. You can't seem to sneak in a pass.

Both your center and power forward are tightly guarded. You don't want to risk turning the ball over, so you look elsewhere. Swinging around behind the defense is your other forward. In a second, he'll be open. But he runs into a hard pick along the baseline. He's no longer an option. Your fellow guard is also unavailable, the victim of a slippery court. He's currently on his back, near the opposing team's bench.

It's up to you to make something happen. Especially since the game is tied with under a minute to play.

You fake like you're going left. But then you quickly put the ball on the floor and dribble to the right. Sweat pours down your forehead. You feel the wind on your face as you cruise past the foul line. Making your way down the lane, you see daylight ahead. So you turn on the jets. You are the fastest player on the court and you know it.

From across the paint comes the weak-side defense. You knew it was coming, so you're ready for the pressure. You expected the hand in your face and the hard bump to your body. Neither tactic will rattle you. You've been here before.

Still, the defensive pressure slows you down. In fact, your momentum is almost completely stopped. That's all right, though, since the defensive switch means someone else is open. So, right before you slam on the brakes, you dish the ball off. Your big man catches the pretty, no-look pass.

With a clean view of the basket, he fires one up. But his short jumper doesn't have enough arc. The ball hits the rim and bounces back toward the ground. A defender barely gets an outstretched fingertip on it. This deflects the rebound in your direction. A moment later, your luck has changed. The ball lands in your lap. Once again, your grip tightens.

There are now five seconds remaining. Before the defense can react, you make a charge at the hoop. The defense collapses. You let go with a short bank shot as the buzzer sounds. In a desperate attempt to keep you from scoring, your opponents foul you hard.

As a result, you end up on the floor, unable to move. You try to make out the numbers on the scoreboard. At first, they are blurry, but they soon come into focus. Time has expired, and your shot didn't go in. The score is still tied.

After being fouled like that, you're going to get another chance. You can win the game by making at least one of two shots at the free-throw line. Now, if you can only find the strength. You need to push yourself off the floor and thrust your body *back into your wheelchair*. Can you imagine that?

For Bryson McLeod, this is a familiar scene. The 16-year-old from New Jersey has been here a number of times. That's because Bryson is a wheelchair basketball player—and a good one, too. He is no stranger to physical contact. After all, he's been playing the sport competitively for several years now.

When you attend a wheelchair basketball game, right away you notice the sound. The noises you hear are strange. The crowd might be loud, just like any other crowd. But what you hear taking place *on* the court sounds different. It's not the familiar squeak of sneakers on the hardwood. That noise is replaced by the sound of metal chairs slamming into each other.

Things can get pretty rough out there. During the course of a game, these mini-crashes occur all the time. For a new fan or player, the noise takes some getting used to. But for experienced ballers like Bryson, it's like beautiful music.

Practice makes perfect: Bryson leads the pack during a loose ball drill.

Wheelchair basketball players are getting to do something they love at a high level. The intensity on the court rivals that of any other basketball game. A person in a wheelchair will tell you the experience is a magical one.

The game of wheelchair basketball is just like the NBA games on TNT. Or the college hoops on ESPN. It is fast-paced and physical. The court looks the same. The jerseys look the same. The game is even played the same way, with the same number of players. The positions are the same, too, and so is the strategy. Sometimes, players hit difficult shots. Sometimes, they choke and miss easy ones. And sometimes, they hit the deck. The only difference: When they get up, they have to get back into their wheelchairs.

Bryson describes the physical demands of wheelchair basketball in an interesting way. He says, "You find out fast how tough you are going full speed in a metal chair. Driving down the lane takes on a whole different meaning when you're on wheels."

You thought the hardwood was slippery in gym shoes? Now imagine playing in a pair of roller skates!

There is much more to this sport than being able to shoot, dribble and pass. To play wheelchair basketball at a high level, you need major upper body strength. You also need to be fearless. A strong sense of strategy and creativity are important, too. The game is so complex because it combines so many different skills.

Danielle Peers of the Canadian national wheelchair basketball team knows this well. She says that these athletes must combine the skill of basketball with the positioning of rugby. They need to do this while playing with the contact required in hockey. And they are sort of like polo players, too. Because just like polo, the game is often played *below* them. Instead of being on horses, though, these basketball players are riding high in their wheelchairs.

Did you know there are about 54 million Americans with disabilities? That number represents about 20 percent of the population, or one in five people. Disabilities range from physical to mental—and from slight to severe. In every case, disabled people face a lifelong challenge. They want to get the most out of themselves despite their handicap. Wheelchair basketball is just one way disabled athletes can feel normal.

Every disability requires something different of the person who has it. For people like Bryson, whose disability requires a wheelchair, life can be a constant struggle. Some of the simple things that others take for granted can be very difficult. For example, getting up and down stairs, or in and out of bed, can require great effort.

Sometimes disabled people have to deal with not fitting in. This can cause heartache, frustration and pain. But is someone in a wheelchair really that different from someone who can stand and walk? Think about it. What's the difference?

In spite of this fact, people in wheelchairs are often stared at. When that's not happening, they're being ignored. Sometimes, people feel sorry for them. Other times, they're on the receiving end of anger. Often, others don't want to change their usual way of doing things to be helpful.

That's part of what makes Bryson McLeod so special. His life is hard. What he endures every day would be enough to get most people down. Yet, he's able to stay positive and excited about life each and every day. Wherever he goes, Bryson brings a smile with him—especially on the hardwood.

Bryson tried several other sports before he found basketball. Each activity gave him an opportunity to overcome his circumstances. His journey is all about his amazing determination. And his goal is to be the very best he can be.

For Bryson, playing competitive sports like wheelchair basketball is an awesome experience. It gives him the chance to be stared at because he's good at something. Not because of the chair he sits in.

Chapter Two

Medical Mystery

Bryson has a serious disease that he was born with. It's called "spina bifida," and it's the most common permanently disabling birth defect in America. (This means that if someone is born with spina bifida, he or she has it forever.) Spina bifida occurs when a baby's spine fails to close all the way during the mother's pregnancy.

The disease strikes about one out of every thousand newborns in the United States. Each new-born is affected in a different way. Unfortunately, doctors and scientists are not sure what causes spina bifida. Currently, there is no cure. The nerve tissue that is damaged or lost because of the disease cannot be repaired or replaced.

It's a terrible disease. It leaves half of the people who have it in a wheelchair. They face a long and hard road. But Bryson McLeod, and many more like him, try not to focus on the negative.

Spend a few minutes with Bryson, and you forget he's even in a wheelchair. You wouldn't know he has been in and out of the hospital for most of his life. His medical condition is not something he's likely to bring up in conversation. He'd rather talk about the sports he plays, his favorite movies and his friends. Or the latest song he learned to play on the piano.

Bryson's disease has in some ways been more difficult for his mother than for him. Finding out your child is disabled can make a parent feel completely helpless.

Bryson's mom's name is Angela Sampson-

McLeod. When she was six months pregnant with Bryson, she visited her doctor for a check-up. They told her to come back for a folic acid test. This is a laboratory test that measures the amount of folic acid in the blood. While everyone needs folic acid, it is especially important for pregnant women. It helps babies to develop normally.

The results of Angela's test were unclear. But her doctor told her to eat more iron, which helps build folic acid. Spinach was her usual source of iron, and she ate it throughout her pregnancy. When she took the test a few weeks later, the results were fine. So she was feeling good about the health of her baby. That is, until she had a sonogram.

A sonogram is a computer picture taken of the mother's stomach. The sonogram she had that day showed a fuzzy area on Bryson's spine. At the time, Angela was told there was nothing to worry about. There wasn't anything that could be done anyway.

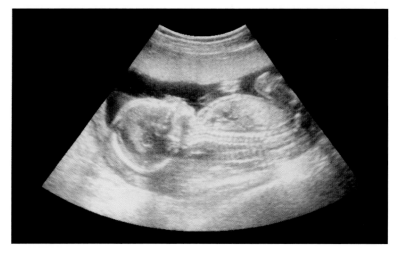

Bryson was sort of a "medical mystery." That's because he never had the regular symptoms of spina bifida. When he was a baby, though, his feet would shake. But the doctors didn't think this was related to spina bifida. Still, they kept Bryson under observation for a few weeks, poking and prodding him. The doctors admitted they were confused. They couldn't figure out what was causing Bryson's feet and legs to shake. Eventually, they told his mom she could take him home. They also told her to keep an eye on his shaking.

Nothing came to light until Bryson started walking. That's when his mom really started to worry. "I could see he wasn't letting go of anything as he was trying to walk. He had no strength in his legs," says his mom. "And he didn't trust himself to see if they would hold him up."

Back at the hospital, more tests finally told the story Angela was afraid of. The fuzzy area on Bryson's spine was crushing nerves from his back to his legs. As it turned out, Bryson was born with a unique kind of spina bifida. And it demanded he go in for surgery.

At the age of 2, little Bryson went under the knife. He had several bones, along with some bad tissue in his back, taken out. In their place, he received titanium rods. (These titanium rods are made of a material similar to that in some golf clubs.)

The recovery from the operation was the worst part for Bryson. He had to lie flat on his back in the hospital for an entire week. A full week without turning over! Luckily, Bryson was upbeat, even at such a young age. His positive approach from the get-go was a huge advantage for him.

When he arrived home the following week, he was barely able to crawl. He needed physical therapy, plus a walker to get him up on his feet again. And then, he needed crutches. The problem was that he hated them. His mother couldn't get Bryson to try his crutches, even for a second. So, she bought him a pair of roller skates instead.

"Apparently, I always wanted them," says Bryson, chuckling.

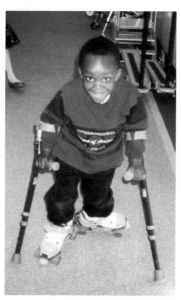

By skating *and* using his crutches for arm support, Bryson slowly worked his way off his walker. In addition, he started swimming to burn off some of his extra energy. At 4 years old, he could swim the length of the pool at the YMCA. That's impressive for someone who has little to no strength in his legs. Next time you are in a pool, try swimming *one* lap without using your legs!

While Bryson seemed to be moving forward, something inside of him just wasn't right. The rods in his back were starting to shift. Once again, the doctors were confused. They'd never seen a kid so active that the rods in his back actually moved. There was just no keeping Bryson still. Yes, he was born with a disease. But he was also born with a motor that never stopped running.

To stop the rods from shifting—and his spine from curving—Bryson needed another operation. This time, the doctors would replace the rods he received at age 2 with new ones. The tendons in his legs would also need to be lengthened, to straighten his legs. (Tendons are bands of tissue that connect muscle to bone.)

At the age of 4, Bryson calmly went into this second surgery. And once again, he amazed the doctors during his recovery. When his casts came off, he started to move his legs right away. Bryson's legs weren't stiff, either, and they *definitely* should have been. Especially after being in casts for such a long time. The doctors were starting to realize how special Bryson was. When it came to this 4 year-old, they could throw their medical books and past experiences out the window.

Chapter Three

Lights, Camera ...

Shortly after that second operation, Bryson's brother Ashby was born. Bryson was 5 at the time. As a divorced, single mother raising two kids, one of whom is disabled, Angela's job is never easy. Once Ashby was born, things got even more complex for her. At this point, Bryson's story also became Ashby's story. That's because you cannot live with a brother in a wheelchair and not be affected.

It's never hard to make Bryson smile. But the arrival of his younger brother made Bryson flash his teeth even more. Sure, over time, it would bother

Bryson when people thought he and Ashby were twins. (Even though Bryson is five years older, they are almost the same height. That's because spina bifida can often slow one's growth.) But that feeling has long since passed.

Bryson poses with his younger brother, Ashby.

Ashby has been more than just a brother to Bryson. He's been his best friend and athletic training partner, too. Now 10 years old, Ashby used to be nervous all the time for Bryson. He worried that his big brother was going to fall out of his wheelchair. He thought Bryson would get injured or be laughed at by other kids. Like his mother, Ashby took his brother's being in a wheelchair harder than Bryson did. He built an invisible fence around his big brother. He wanted to keep others from getting too close to

Bryson, fearing he'd get hurt.

"Ashby is Bryson's protector, even though he's the younger brother," says their mom. "He's the first to pick him up when he falls. I've had to tell him that it's okay if people touch his brother. Before, if someone got too close to Bryson, Ashby would jump in between them."

Ashby remembers one day, when the two boys were visiting their father: Bryson fell while riding his specially designed, four-wheeled dirt bike. "I knew it was going to happen," says Ashby. "But I didn't say anything. Bryson always goes 100 percent. He never slows down. He wouldn't want me to stop him. He'd say something like, 'I don't stop you from falling, so don't stop me.'"

When they're together, they're just like any other pair of brothers. Ashby, who started taking karate classes at 4 1/2 years old, is now a black belt. He will often try out his new kickboxing moves on Bryson. He also helps out at Bryson's basketball practices. When the team needs an extra man, he climbs into a wheelchair and plays. Without the use of his legs, Ashby can experience the game his brother plays. Once seated in that chair, Ashby can see just how hard the sport is.

Neither Bryson nor Ashby is content sitting still. The two of them are always doing something. It could be battling it out in ping pong or shooting hoops. Or it could be playing the piano or challenging each other in PlayStation. Competing is at the heart of their special relationship.

"Ashby's a good brother," says Bryson. Then he smiles slightly, "I mean, he isn't perfect, but he's always there for me."

Bryson's smile is the one constant in the McLeod family's life. It's the reason people seem to flock to him. Sure, he's a bit quiet at first, like most kids are. But before long, he flashes that toothy grin. And it's as if a window to his soul has been opened. His sense of humor and easygoing attitude shine right through.

That grin is also what got him a job as a child model. He was only 4 years old when he started! Even at his young age, Bryson was beyond being self-conscious. He had no issue with getting in front of the camera, even though he had a disability.

"Bryson is just so smart," says his former physical therapist, Dolores D'Andrea. "When I first looked into his eyes, I knew he was special. Plus, I could see that he was comfortable in his own skin. That's why he was able to step in front of the camera so easily."

In 1996, Bryson and his mom were living in Garfield, New Jersey. Bryson was restless. His energy was high despite the leg braces and arm crutches he had to use. This energy needed to be released some*how*—and into some*thing*.

At the time, that thing turned out to be modeling. It all started at Bryson's physical therapy office in the nearby town of Hackensack. The office gave his mom information about a casting director who had stopped by. He was looking for new talent. Everyone at the therapist's office had immediately thought of Bryson. The director and camera crew would be coming back the next day, they said. Why don't Bryson and his mother check them out?

The two agreed to stop by, although neither knew what to expect. The casting director liked Bryson right away. His smile was what first got him noticed. Yet, it was his upbeat personality that sealed the deal.

After that first experience in front of the camera, many modeling opportunities came Bryson's way. During the next few years, he posed for magazines, in-store posters and newspaper fliers. Over time, he worked for companies like Toys "R" Us, Foot Locker and Nike.

Bryson doesn't remember much about his modeling days. He does recall, though, that everyone always seemed to crowd around him. And that he made the grown-ups laugh.

"The photographers were always happy when they saw Bryson," says his mom. "They never had to prompt him to smile. They knew that, with Bryson, they would have an easy day."

But soon, posing in front of the camera just wasn't enough action for Bryson. As always, his mind was moving quickly and he wanted his body to follow. He had too much energy and too much athletic ability to waste them. He knew he could accomplish great things in sports if given the opportunity.

You see, Bryson always focuses on what *can* be achieved, not on what can't. This is never truer than when he's competing. He loves being in the spotlight, in the center of the action, going full speed ahead.

Chapter Four

Lightning on Ice

Bryson's mother was born and raised on the Caribbean island of Trinidad. The island is located between the Caribbean Sea and the Atlantic Ocean. It is northeast of Venezuela.

Beautiful Maracas Bay, Trinidad...no ice in sight!

Sports in Trinidad reflect the nation's British influence. Cricket, a bat-and-ball game similar to baseball, is the top sport. Soccer is a close second. Both outdoor sports are played under the warm, tropical sun. And in Trinidad, the sun shines brightly nearly year-round. Being located in the tropics, one thing the nation doesn't see much of is ice.

So when Angela decided to let her son try the sport of sled hockey, it was brand-new to her. She knew next to nothing about hockey and certainly didn't know what to think of sled hockey! Neither did Bryson.

The sport of sled hockey was invented in Sweden. (Sometimes it's still called "sledge" hockey, which is what the Swedes originally named it.) A group of patients invented the game at a rehab center in the early 1960s. Even though they were disabled, the patients still wanted to play hockey. This led the Swedes to create a new sport, based on hockey. The men built a metal-framed sled, or sledge, with two ice hockey skate blades. They used round poles with bike handles for sticks. And they played without goaltenders on a frozen lake near Stockholm, the capital of Sweden.

The sport caught on very quickly. By 1969, Stockholm had a five-team league. It included both physically disabled and non-disabled players. That same year, Stockholm hosted the first international sledge hockey match. It was between a local club team and one from Norway. During the 1970s, teams from these two countries played once or twice a year. Soon, other countries began to establish teams. The United States fielded its first international squad in 1990. And the sport continues to grow in popularity to this day.

Two Swedish national teams played an exhibition match in 1976. It was at the first Paralympic Winter Games, held in Sweden. The Paralympics are similar to the Olympics. They are a multi-sport, multinational event. But, their participants are athletes with physical and mental disabilities. Eighteen years after that exhibition match, sledge hockey became an official event at the 1994 Paralympics in Norway—which was a pretty big deal.

Athletes compete in this sport while sitting on a sled. Made of either aluminum or steel, the sled is about 4 feet long. Its front end is curved, while its back contains a seat, or bucket.

The entire sled is set on top of two regular-sized ice hockey skate blades. The blades themselves cannot be longer than a third of the length of the sled. The height of the frame has to allow for the puck to pass beneath it. This way, the puck doesn't constantly bump up against sleds and come to a stop.

These regulations make a lot of sense. To level the playing field, everyone needs to follow the same rules, just like in Motocross or NASCAR. In those sports, materials—including the engines themselves—are strictly regulated. Any sport in that uses sophisticated equipment must be strict about that equipment. No one player should have an advantage over any other. Plus, safety must be guaranteed. That's why in sled hockey, straps are used to secure players' feet, ankles, knees and hips to the sled.

In traditional hockey, each player carries one long wooden stick. But in sled hockey, players use two sticks. These sticks are each about one-third the size of a regulation hockey stick. They have a hooked wooden blade at one end, similar to a regular hockey stick. This is for puck handling, passing and shooting. But the other end has a pick, used to move oneself across the ice. It is similar to a toe pick at the front of a figure skate blade. Its teeth, while sharp, cannot damage the ice surface or accidentally slash other players. Skilled players must be able to quickly switch ends of the stick during play. The best players can go from passing or shooting, to skating, in the blink of an eye.

Besides these differences, the rules basically copy those of the International Ice Hockey Federation. Six players per team are allowed on the ice at one time. There's a goaltender, two defensemen, two wings and one center.

There are some minor penalties found in sled hockey that are not found in traditional hockey. They include using an illegally sized stick and carrying the pick end above the waist. Using the pick end of the stick near an opponent is also not allowed. Neither is ramming an opponent or lifting the underside of the sled or trapping the puck.

Major penalties are similar to hockey's five-minute majors (for fighting, boarding and spearing). They include pushing a player from behind with one's stick and throwing the stick. Drawing blood with the pick end of the stick is also a major penalty. So is using any other attempt to injure another player on purpose.

Bryson McLeod entered South Mountain Arena in West Orange, New Jersey, in the fall of 2000. (This was way before he discovered wheelchair basketball.) As he did, he knew he was in for an experience like no other. The arena was originally built to offer ice skating to the general public. In 1986, it became the training facility for the New Jersey Devils hockey team. At the time, the New Jersey Devils Youth Hockey Club practiced and played there, too. And so did their affiliate sled hockey team.

The inside of the building was cold when Bryson arrived to try out sled hockey. It was a sport he had never seen before. From his first glance at the ice, Bryson could tell that playing would be lots of fun. Bryson was 8 years old at the time—and the smallest kid at South Mountain Arena that day! But that didn't bother him. He was too excited to be nervous.

He watched the action from behind the Plexiglas surrounding the ice. The sled hockey team was practicing that day, and Bryson was in awe. He watched a winger juke a defender and send a crossing pass. Skating onto it was the Devils' center. He blasted a slap shot past the extended glove of the goaltender. The puck moved so fast it could barely be seen whizzing by. Bryson guessed that the shot must have been around 100 miles per hour. "Awesome," he whispered.

Next, he watched as the team practiced defending against the power play. He studied how to check an opponent into the boards. And he learned what to do to score on a breakaway. After a few minutes, all he wanted was to get out on the ice. He was ready to show what he could do. But it wasn't easy. Skating up and down the ice on that sled was difficult. Bryson had trouble moving at all, let alone in any specific direction.

"I remember it was very hard at first," says Bryson. "Relying on my upper body strength, which I didn't have much of, was tough. Plus, I wasn't used to using the sticks to move myself forward. The moment I started in the right direction, the puck would be hit toward me. Then, I'd use the wrong side of the stick to try to hit it. I can't imagine how bad I looked that first day."

That first day was rough, but Bryson showed

improvement every minute he was out there. It didn't take him long to figure out how to use his sticks. Soon, he was able to propel himself down the ice. He also learned how to flip his stick in order to move, shoot and pass.

After a few weeks, Bryson really started to get the hang of this new sport. During his first scrimmage, a loose puck landed near the far boards. He took off toward it like a rocket. This was his first real test out on the ice. He desperately wanted to ace it. He thrust himself forward with everything he had. A defender from the opposing team had taken off at the exact same moment. They were in an all-out race down the ice. Whoever got there first would win the puck.

The boys raced side-by-side, neither gaining on

the other. Bryson made a quick strategic maneuver when he was about 20 feet from the wall. He slowed down. He wanted his opponent to get a few feet in front of him. It worked perfectly.

The moment the kid's stick touched that puck, Bryson barreled into him. It was a fierce body check, the first of his sled hockey career. And boy did it feel good! Bryson quickly grabbed control of the puck and slapped it over to a teammate. A huge smile came to his face. Bryson was starting to realize that he liked the contact of sled hockey.

"In most games, I'd start by going after the biggest guy out there," says Bryson. "Even though he might get the better of me, I'd be sending a message. Once the other team knows you're not scared, the game gets easier. Most times, I'd get beat up a little, and my mom would be pretty scared. But I was getting stronger, faster and more coordinated with the puck every day."

As it turned out, Bryson enjoyed hitting, and getting hit, although that didn't happen often. Shortly after showing up at South Mountain Arena, Bryson became his team's fastest player. In fact, he was usually the fastest player on the ice. Folks in the stands started giving him nicknames in honor of his speed. They'd chant these names as he skated down the ice to score another goal.

"Speedy," "Speed Demon," "Little Flea" and "Lightning on Ice" were just some of his nicknames.

"Being small and quick makes you a fan favorite, I guess," Bryson says.

Bryson realized something about himself rather quickly. While modeling definitely put him in the spotlight, hockey did so much more for him. The sport gave Bryson the opportunity to be the "go-to guy." He accepted the role happily. On the ice, he enjoyed pushing himself and testing the limits of his disability. He worked hard to be a better athlete, a good teammate and a leader. More than anything else, though, he just loved playing.

Although he knew nothing about the sport at first, he quickly excelled. With the help of some more experienced teammates, he learned all the little things about sledge hockey. (One of his former teammates was so good that he is now a member of the United States National Sled Hockey Team. Still, it was often Bryson's name being yelled by the fans.)

Bryson remembers one of his greatest games from early on in his sled hockey career. His squad was playing a team called the Wings of Steel. He was 10, and as usual, one of the youngest and smallest on the ice. But he was on fire that day. He blew by the defense to score three goals, his first "hat trick."

Be it practice or a game, Bryson never wanted to leave the ice. He loved the sport so much that he said good-bye to the fame and fortune of modeling. He wanted to focus his energy entirely on sled hockey.

"I put it to Bryson clearly," his mother recalls.

"I said, 'If you continue modeling, they pay us. If you play sled hockey, we pay them.'" She laughs as she remembers the look on Bryson's face. It was clear that he saw himself as an athlete who had modeled. Not as a model who played sports. His days in front of the camera were over. But his days in the limelight had just begun.

Chapter Five

On Your Mark, Get Set, Go!

Today, nearly 75 percent of people born with spina bifida compete in sports and other recreational activities. Just as with non-disabled kids, these activities help young people develop social and motor skills. At the same time, they learn how to be members of a team.

Bryson was consumed with sled hockey for several years. He enjoyed the thrill of gliding down the ice and slamming someone into the boards. Yet, despite his success in the sport, something inside of him told him it wasn't enough. He needed more.

At the time, he didn't know that a new activity was around the corner. But he'd soon find out. Jimmy Cuevas, a local wheelchair track and field coach, spotted Bryson at sled hockey practice. He noticed how athletic Bryson was as he flew down the ice.

Coach Cuevas saw an opportunity to improve his track and field team. He invited Bryson to check out one of *his* training sessions. And the rest, as they say, is history.

Track and field called out to Bryson from the very first time he tried it. He soon realized that this sport was very different from sled hockey. But it provided an equally awesome challenge. As always, the appeal of something new drew him in.

There was little contact in track, which Bryson had grown to love in playing sled hockey. No, track didn't offer him much in the "crunch and punch" category. But it made up for that in other ways. It allowed Bryson to put his speed, strength and endurance to the ultimate test.

What makes track so unique is that there is no defense to react to. There's no ball to bounce or puck to maneuver. Success depends entirely on the competitor and how hard he is willing to push himself. Because of this, many people refer to track as "the ultimate test." In track, Bryson would be able to search deep within himself. He would find out the true limits—and reach—of his body.

Soon, he was working out with the local United Spinal Association wheelchair sports team. Called the North Jersey Navigators, the squad is based in Jersey City. Bryson put everything he had into his training sessions. Soon, he was participating in sprints, middle distance, long distance and relay races. He also tried throwing events, like the discus, shot put and javelin.

Above, Bryson hurls the discus.

These events are the same as those offered at the Paralympic Games. He hopes to compete in the Paralympics one day, but getting there won't be easy.

Making the United States Paralympic roster is just as difficult as making the Olympic team.

But Bryson is one step closer than most. Last year, he was invited to join the Team USA track and field squad. Being on this team, which competes internationally, will be a great experience. Bryson will be able to compete against other top athletes around the world! He hopes it will better prepare him to qualify for the Paralympics.

As in sled hockey, wheelchair athletes in track and field have to follow specific rules. One fairly obvious one is that they cannot use a motorized wheelchair. In relays, they don't carry a baton, so they must touch their partner. In throwing events, their wheelchairs must be firmly attached to the ground. And they must remain seated until the discus, javelin or shot put is released. Finally, they cannot have any part of their body touch the ground.

Already a proven athlete, Bryson started to shine on the track almost immediately. He competed for the first time at 10, in an indoor meet in Connecticut. He came in second in every event he entered that day. And that was despite being in a special track wheelchair for the very first time.

These wheelchairs look more like three-wheeled bicycles. Extended rims on each side wheel provide a better grip for athletes to "run." (Non-disabled sprinters use their feet to dash. Wheelchair sprinters grab their wheels with their hands and spin.) The entire chair has a sleek design and is built for speed.

Competing in one of these chairs for the first time was tricky for Bryson. The fact that he *still* managed to finish in second place says a lot about his athletic ability.

Bryson remembers those early races. While waiting for the starting gun to go off, he would glance over at his fellow competitors. Most were more experienced than he was. But he had a drive and a determination that helped him fly down the track.

Sometimes, Bryson would get so focused that it seemed like someone had turned off the rest of the world. While in this zone, everything would get quiet. In these moments, it was just Bryson and his wheelchair, challenging both time and space. Sometimes, all he could hear was his heart beating as he sprinted ahead. Once Bryson crossed the finish line, the sounds around him would return to his ears. More often than not, they were cheers—and they were for him.

As time went on, racing became second nature, and Bryson found even more success. In May 2007, he came in fifth in a 1600-meter race in New York. This was special because Bryson, a high school freshman at the time, raced against mostly seniors.

"Bryson has shown he can pick up the basics of any wheelchair track event. And then, he quickly excels at it," says Coach Cuevas, who's been with Bryson since 2003. "He's a good athlete with an excellent future ahead of him. He can become one of the best in the country in his division."

In July 2007, Bryson and his mom boarded a plane for the Pacific Northwest. Their destination: the National Junior Disability Championships in Spokane, Washington. There, Bryson competed in nine events in track and field, as well as table tennis. He netted a total of eight medals—four silver and four bronze. He was also part of the Navigators relay team, which won two gold medals.

This performance added to an already impressive string of gold, silver and bronze medals. Bryson earned them at various regional, tri-state and national competitions. In 2003, 2004 and 2006, Bryson won gold in the shot, discus, javelin and track. Quite an impressive record!

But going from excellent sled hockey player to premier track and field star wasn't enough. Even the ping pong championships he won didn't provide him with the rush he was craving. Despite all his success, Bryson felt that something was missing for him athletically. And he was sure he hadn't quite found his calling yet.

"Don't get me wrong. I love track and I love sled hockey. I love them both for different reasons," Bryson says. "In sled hockey, the contact and the team aspect are awesome. And track is *the* way to see how far you can push yourself. It's not really a team sport, though," he adds. "When you add up the points at meets, the final score is the team score. But at the same time, most events are individual. I like the team aspect more, which is why I enjoy the relays the most."

Bryson started looking for a combination of what he got on the ice *and* the track. To this day, he still competes in both these sports. But some of his track teammates convinced him, at 12, to try a new sport. It has now become his favorite one of all: basketball.

Bryson has earned quite a collection of medals and awards over the years.

Chapter Six

On the Hardwood

In 2003, the McLeods moved from Garfield, New Jersey, to the town of Wood-Ridge. Wood-Ridge is down the road from the Izod Center, home to the NBA's New Jersey Nets. With basketball being Bryson's new number one priority, the relocation made perfect sense. That's because Bryson plays basketball with the United Spinal Junior Nets.

The team is co-sponsored by the United Spinal Association and the NBA franchise. Ranked ninth in the nation in 2008, the team plays all over the Northeast. In 2005 and 2006, the Junior Nets won the

National Wheelchair Basketball Association Prep League National Championship.

The United Spinal Junior Nets went undefeated at the 2006 Nationals, held in Peoria, Illinois. The tournament featured the top 16 wheelchair basketball teams from around the country. They defended their title with a 38-34 victory over the Sterling Heights (Michigan) Challengers.

Bryson was voted to the tournament's first team. His teammate and longtime friend Dylan Levine was voted Most Valuable Player. Dylan has a disorder that weakens bones, making them brittle. He and Bryson met on the ice at South Mountain Arena when they were 8. At the time, they were the two newest additions to the Devils sled hockey team. Since then, they've played a ton of hockey together. They use their knowledge of each other's playing style to form a dynamic duo on the court. "We've been playing so long together, we could play blindfolded," says Bryson.

Being teammates helps Bryson and Dylan play with confidence. Anyone who's ever played basketball knows you must play with a positive attitude. All great players have it—a certain "swagger." It helps them to play without any hesitation. Even in the NBA, shots just don't fall for players who don't believe in themselves. Luckily, Bryson has never been short on confidence. The major force behind his success has been Bryson's deep belief in his abilities.

Confidence is a key ingredient in most success

stories. But for a disabled person, believing in oneself is not as easy as it sounds. Living each day in a world built for people without disabilities can be downright discouraging. Nearly everything you come across has been constructed for a non-disabled person. Daily life for an individual in a wheelchair can be a series of frustrating experiences. Wheelchair-*un*friendly staircases make certain areas off-limits. Bathroom sinks are too high to use while sitting. Narrow doorways don't let wheelchairs through. Beaches often have no paved walkways.

Staircases like these are not a pretty sight for a person in a wheelchair.

Kitchen tables, beds, schools, restaurants—the list of wheelchair-unfriendly things is long. And whenever one travels via wheelchair, the struggle continues. That's why Bryson's ability to stay confident is so amazing. He does it even though the world seems to have been built to leave him out.

That same "can-do" attitude is what keeps Bryson in the gym after practice. He takes shot after shot to improve his game. His progress on the hardwood is a direct result of his hard work and dedication.

"In the beginning, I couldn't shoot," he says. "I didn't have enough arm power to get the ball in the basket. It's all about upper body strength, and I couldn't even hit the rim. It was like hockey all over again. I had to start from scratch."

As determined as ever, Bryson launched headfirst into his new endeavor. "At first, I wasn't fast because I hadn't figured out the rhythm of the game. And I didn't know how to move the heavier chair that's used in basketball. It's a lot different than the lightweight track chair. Plus, I had to learn how to dribble while moving in all directions. Over time—and after a lot of practice—I adjusted. Now, I'm one of the best ball handlers and shooters on the team. And I'm one of the quickest, too.

"Basketball is the sport I can really see myself excelling in," adds Bryson. (In the summer of 2007, he attended basketball camp with his team at the University of Illinois.) "I especially love the team aspect of it," he continues. "An opponent could have quicker players and better shooters than we do. But we can beat them by playing great team basketball."

Wheelchair basketball was originally developed in the mid-1940s by U.S. World War II veterans. Many of these soldiers had come back home from bloody battles overseas with serious injuries. Some were unable to walk. When they discovered they could still compete athletically while in their wheelchairs, several became hooked on wheelchair basketball.

The U.S. Marine Memorial in Washington D.C., depicts perhaps the most famous scene of World War II.

With few exceptions, the rules of wheelchair basketball are the same as those used in the NCAA. The game is played on a regulation-size court. And the baskets are the same height as those used in Division I college ball.

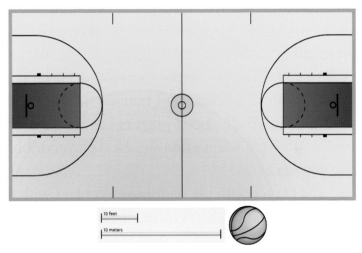

10 feet

10 meters

But in wheelchair basketball, players are given a point value, depending on their functional abilities. The values go from 0.5 (most severely disabled) to 4.5. Among the five players on the court, the overall team point total cannot exceed 12. This means the team has players with many different types and levels of disabilities.

As expected, there are regulations regarding the equipment used during play. In this case, that means the wheelchair. For instance, the height of the seat must not exceed 21 inches from the floor. And the seat cushion can be no more than 4 inches thick.

Fouls are pretty much the same as those in the

NCAA. There are differences, though. A foul can be called when a chair is blocking or charging into another chair. In other words, the chair is considered to be part of the player.

An offensive player cannot remain more than four seconds in the free-throw lane while his or her team has the ball. And players may only push their wheelchair twice before dribbling or passing. If more, they'll be called for a traveling violation. A player may, however, wheel the chair and bounce the ball at the same time. More advanced players can do this. This action is similar to when a non-disabled player dribbles while running.

If a player with the ball makes contact with the floor, it is a violation. So is tilting the chair backward, allowing the standard safety device to touch the floor. In both cases, the ball is awarded to the other team. A player is out of bounds when his or her body or wheelchair goes over the line.

The rule of remaining firmly seated in the chair at all times is strictly enforced. This is so one player does not have an unfair advantage over any other. Breaking this rule—especially on a shot or rebound—is a physical advantage foul. Two free throws are awarded, and the ball is given to the opposing team. A player with three physical advantage infractions "fouls out" of the game.

If a player falls out of the chair during a game, play is immediately suspended. But only if there is a threat of danger to the fallen player. If not, the referees won't blow their whistles until the play is over. If a player falls on purpose to gain possession, the ball is awarded to the opposing team.

Bryson has fallen out of his chair more times than he can count. It was scary at first. But now it's all just part of the game. Like playing with broken fingers, which is common due to opponents' wheelchairs slamming into him.

"In my opinion, basketball is the most physical of the wheelchair sports," says Jose Garcia. He not only coaches Bryson but also plays for the United Spinal Nets adult squad. "These are top-notch athletes going at each other, banging chairs. It's not what some may think is just a recreational activity for handicapped people. It's real basketball."

Don't let anyone tell you wheelchair basketball players aren't tough. They're a lot like sled hockey players. Actually, all wheelchair athletes have to be ready to endure a ton of injuries. Some are well beyond those suffered by non-disabled athletes. Cuts and bruises brought on by collisions are always present. Shoulder pain and rotator cuff (muscles and tendons around the shoulder) strains are regular results of upper body overuse. Pressure sores, caused by sitting in one position for a long time, are also common.

With all that to deal with, some wheelchair athletes barely even notice the blisters. Spinning the wheels of their chairs hard and fast can cause horribly severe blisters. Like other competitors, wheelchair athletes have to play through the pain if they want to excel.

"Once, I didn't even know my finger was broken," says Bryson about a collision. "It hurt pretty badly, but the game was close. So I taped it to the one next to it and kept playing. It was ugly, but I've been through worse than a broken finger."

Chapter Seven

Inspiration

Monday, December 13, 2004.

Angela Sampson-McLeod remembers the day as if it were yesterday. The holidays were right around the corner. It seemed like the whole world was in a good mood. But not Angela. Not on this day. She was biting her fingernails in the waiting room of New York-Presbyterian Children's Hospital.

Outside, the city was alive with activity. Children were playing in the parks. Men and women were on their way to work. Shoppers were trying to buy

last-minute gifts before the holiday rush. Inside the hospital, though, Angela was sitting … waiting … and worrying. A few feet away, behind a closed door, was her 12-year-old son. Bryson was undergoing complicated and life-threatening surgery. This latest operation was to correct his severe scoliosis. Scoliosis is a condition that involves an unnatural curving of the spine. In Bryson's case, it was brought on by his spina bifida.

From 8 o'clock in the morning until 8 o'clock at night, Angela sat there. The surgery took a full 12 hours. Every once in a while, a doctor or nurse would come and talk with her. But, for the most part, she just watched the clock and waited.

Long after dark, Bryson's mom finally heard the news she was praying for. Her son had made it— again. "Bryson's a fighter," says Angela. "From the day he was born, he's overcome adversity. And somehow, he's always done it with a smile on his face."

Angela had known that Bryson would need to have another operation. The titanium rods in his back would need to be replaced. But Bryson's doctors figured it would be when he was older—not at 12. They hadn't predicted that some of his spinal bones would need to come out. The curve in his spine was beginning to fuse. Again, when it came to Bryson, the doctors' prior experiences could be thrown out the window.

The operation had two parts. First, Bryson's surgeons had to go in through his side to take out the fused bones. Then, they had to go in through his back to put in new rods. Just as it was when he was a baby, his recovery was slow and painful. Bryson lost a lot of weight, eventually having to take pills to help him eat. He had to learn the simple things all over again, like how to sit up. Not exactly something an active teenager would want to go through.

This surgery put him on the sidelines for 18 months. It also cost him a full year of school. Plus, it confined him exclusively to a wheelchair. (Until then, Bryson only needed the wheelchair when traveling long distances—or when playing sports.)

Constantly sitting makes it harder for Bryson to straighten his back. Furthermore, because he doesn't use them, his leg muscles are wasting away. But Bryson has never shied away from a challenge. Each procedure he has undergone is a test of his strength, endurance and faith. And none has stopped him from doing the things he loves.

It's not a foregone conclusion that Bryson will be in a wheelchair forever. No way. Bryson wants to get up on crutches again soon. He's already begun his rehab. He's working out on the treadmill and is using weights to strengthen his legs. Sure, he may have to get the tendons in his legs lengthened yet again. But walking is the goal he's aiming for.

Bryson plans on walking again one day soon.

Betting against him would not be wise. Because when Bryson puts his mind to it, he accomplishes great things.

For example, just check out his weekly schedule. He has a pair of physical therapy sessions, one on Tuesdays and one on Thursdays. Plus, he has basketball on Wednesdays and Saturdays, and piano lessons on Thursday evenings (after therapy). Finally, he participates in track and field on Fridays and Sundays. It's a schedule that rivals any other kid's on the block.

sun   mon   tue

1   2   3   4   5

8   9   10   11

15   16   17   18

24   25

Actually, Bryson is busier than most people. And when you're as busy as Bryson, there's no time to feel sorry for yourself. "People find it hard to believe, but my disability is not something I think about. Maybe if I had a lot of time on my hands, I would," he says. "But I don't spend time thinking about what might have been. It is what it is. I handle it, and I move forward."

It's a great attitude—and one that Bryson has maintained for most of his life. Bryson has never really gotten too down about being born with spina bifida. Not even when he lost some of his hair following his latest surgery. In fact, there was only one time when the frustration got the better of him.

For some reason, the mall was a really hard place for Bryson to go. Everyone always seemed to be staring at him. On one occasion, he decided to find out what they were looking at. After catching a group of young people gawking at him, he approached them. He asked what it was that they found so interesting. He wasn't trying to be rude; he actually wanted to know. As they stood in front of him silently, he continued asking questions. "So, what is it about me that makes you stare? Is it the wheelchair? Is there something you'd like to ask me?"

They ran away. They were unwilling to talk to him—or to even look him in the eye. Bryson was left sitting there alone, without an apology or an explanation. It was pretty upsetting, but he didn't dwell on it.

His mom could tell he had let it go. She overheard him on his cell phone with a female friend later that same day. This girl, a high school classmate, was really down and not feeling good about herself. Bryson spoke in a comforting voice, "Look, I'm in a wheelchair—and I'm smiling." He chuckled into the phone, "I'm laughing right now! You're pretty, you're smart, and you've got lots of friends. …"

To that girl, as well as many other people, Bryson is an inspiration.

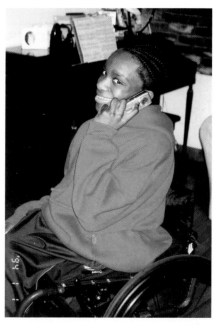

Of course, every disabled person *must* reflect on his or her situation occasionally. Bryson wouldn't be human if somewhere deep down he didn't wonder "what if." The reason Bryson is such a success is that he *has* asked that question. But he's okay with having received no answer. And he's moved on with even more determination.

As a toddler, Bryson thought he was the only one in the world like him. At 3 years old, he asked a question that disabled people have always asked: "Why was I born like this?" It was a question nobody could answer—not even his mother. Instead, she let Bryson know it was up to him not to be cast aside. It was his choice not to be overlooked, not to be taken advantage of. And not to be sad. He has definitely taken his mother's advice.

"Bryson is upbeat about everything," says Re Marks, one of Bryson's basketball coaches. "Although he takes his basketball seriously, he helps keep everyone loose. He's a funny kid who brings some comic relief to the team."

Bryson keeps his family smiling, too. Ashby says that, although his brother is funny, he doesn't know when to stop talking. "Bryson starts telling a story on a Thursday and, by the time he finishes, it's Friday."

At this point, Bryson smiles, "If I weren't in this house, no one would laugh. End of story."

For Bryson, going to school has had its ups and downs. Not in the classroom, though. Bryson is doing just fine with his studies.

After years of searching for the right school, his mom found the Hackensack Christian School. There, Bryson went through the eighth grade in a close-knit and supportive environment. He fit right in. Of course, there was a period of adjustment. Bryson remembers having to tell his new classmates that he was just like them. Except that he couldn't walk like they did.

He recalls falling off the stage once while singing in a school concert. He laughed right along with his mom and brother when they called him "Humpty Dumpty." It was then that his classmates finally got it. Bryson was just another kid, more like them than they had originally thought. He could poke fun at himself when he did something dumb, just like they did. He was in a wheelchair some of the time—that's all. No big deal.

What has been difficult over the years, though, is getting to and from school. When Bryson was little, his mom would push him in a stroller. But, as he grew, she couldn't do it anymore. He became too big and heavy for her. And it didn't get all that much easier when he moved to a wheelchair. She and Ashby would have to lift the chair into the car once Bryson was inside.

Bryson could have stayed at Hackensack Christian through high school. But he needed special transportation as he got bigger. So he transferred to Wood-Ridge High School.

That's because the bus Bryson now takes every morning to Wood-Ridge High has a lift. Bryson wheels himself onto a platform, which rises up. Then, he rolls himself on board. This helps him to be more self-sufficient.

After eight years at Hackensack, Bryson was fine with the move to a new school. Sure, he only knew three kids upon arriving at Wood-Ridge High. But he was confident he'd quickly make new friends, which he did.

Hanging out with friends at a Sweet 16 party.

His life is very similar to the lives of his class-mates. In fact, it is more similar than most people would imagine. After school, he does his homework, goes online, talks on the phone and plays video games. It's the little things that are different.

For example, getting ready for school is a little

different for Bryson. Upon waking, he pulls himself from his bed to a chair. Once there, he gets dressed. Then, he crawls to the top of the stairs. He makes his way down on his butt, using his arms to descend each step. Waiting for him at the bottom of the staircase is his wheelchair.

Bathing in the downstairs bathroom isn't so bad. Bryson moves right from his wheelchair to a seat inside the shower. Upstairs isn't as easy. There's a tub in the second-floor bathroom, so Bryson needs his brother's help. Ashby has to lift him over the side. While his mom looks to install another roll-in shower stall, Bryson carries on.

He uses the ramp behind his house to enter the kitchen from outdoors. He climbs the stairs the same way he comes down them—on his butt. And in the event of a fire, he knows what to do. He's practiced throwing a soft ladder out his second-floor bedroom window. Once on it, Bryson can slide down to safety.

"When I'm doing my daily activities, I feel like any non-disabled person," says Bryson. "Maybe it takes me a little longer to do some routine things. But I see no difference. None at all. And that's how I think about it."

Like many other athletes, Bryson has a shed out back with all his gear. Another little difference, though: Bryson's equipment is expensive—really expensive. He's got all his wheelchairs out there, different ones for the various sports he plays. They're in addition to the everyday chair he uses at school and around the house. And as he grows older, and bigger, he will constantly need new wheelchairs.

That's where his mom comes in. Having appointed herself Bryson's "agent," she serves her client well. Her letter-writing efforts once landed Bryson a free racing chair for track. And she's constantly looking for ways to pay for his equipment, training fees and travel expenses.

Angela stays on the lookout for donations and sponsors. They're the only way Bryson can continue to compete in the sports he loves. On average, each trip he takes to a tournament or meet is around $5,000. That includes the cost of registration fees, transportation, van rentals, lodging and meals. Lately, his need for funding has become even more important. That's because he's got his sights set on the Paralympics.

Chapter 8

The Paralympics and Beyond

The idea for today's Paralympic Games was born in 1948. Sir Ludwig Guttman, a German-born doctor, organized a sports competition in England. It involved World War II veterans with spinal cord injuries. The event was a great success. Four years later, athletes from the Netherlands joined, and word began to spread.

In 1960, in Rome, these Olympic-style games for disabled athletes officially went global. The 9th Annual International Stoke Mandeville Games were under way. This event became known as the first Paralympic Games. Sixteen years later, in Toronto, other disability groups were added to the event. In that same year, 1976, the first *official* Paralympic Winter Games took place in Sweden.

Today, the Paralympics are an elite global sporting event for athletes from six different disability groups. (Wheelchair is just one of the categories.) The Games stress the athletes' achievements rather than their disabilities. The movement has grown dramatically since its first days. For example, the number of individuals participating in the Summer Paralympic Games has increased greatly. In 1960, 400 athletes represented 23 countries. In 2004, nearly 4,000 folks from 136 countries competed.

The Paralympic Games are always held the same year as the Olympic Games. Since 1988, they have also been in the same place as the Olympics. Starting in 2012, the city chosen to host the Olympics *must* also host the Paralympics. The Summer Games feature 20 sports, while the Winter Games highlight five. Bryson plays some of the most popular ones of all.

Track and field events at the Paralympics attract the greatest number of both athletes *and* spectators. Some athletes compete in wheelchairs. Others use prostheses (artificial devices used to replace missing arms and legs). Even blind athletes compete, with the help of a sighted guide.

There are lots of other events. For example, table tennis was there at the first Paralympic Games in 1960. In 2006, it was played by athletes from 104 different countries. Men and women compete individually, in doubles, and in team events, either standing or sitting. A match is five sets of 11 points each. The winner is the player—or pair—who wins the best out of five sets.

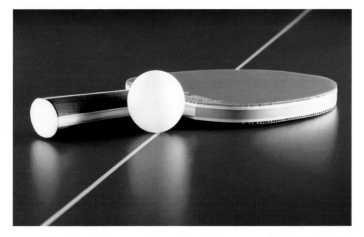

Sled hockey arrived in Norway in 1994. Since then, it has quickly become one of the hottest tickets at the Winter Paralympics. In 2006, it was played by athletes from 12 countries.

Wheelchair basketball was formally introduced to the Paralympic program in Rome in 1960. It is one of the most popular sports in the Games. In 2006, it was played by athletes from 77 countries.

Bryson's hope is to compete in one of the above events, basketball in particular. He's well on his way to reaching that dream. He's faced athletes from all over the United States and abroad. And he's already started his difficult training for the move up in competition.

Each year, Bryson competes with the North Jersey Navigators in seven major track competitions. He does so in order to qualify for the annual National

Junior Disability Championships.

In 2008, the week-long event took place in New Jersey, at Rutgers University. Fortunately, Bryson didn't have to make another expensive cross-country trip to participate. In the future, though, Bryson will need to travel even more than in the past. He must, if he wants to showcase his talent against the best competition. He'll most likely have to return to several of the places he's traveled to before. (Bryson has already been to Arizona, Washington, Illinois, Alabama, Oklahoma, Nebraska and Florida.) He'll also probably need to visit some new states. And if Bryson makes it to the Paralympics, he'll become a world traveler.

Planning for the future is difficult for any kid, but especially for Bryson. There are just so many sports he loves and excels in. He has even thought about giving wheelchair boxing a shot. "You need upper body strength and then some," he says. "But maybe I could be the next Floyd Mayweather."

Recently, Bryson even tried wheelchair rugby. This full-contact sport received attention thanks to the award-winning 2005 film *Murderball*. The movie shatters the myth that paralyzed men and women in wheelchairs can't control their limbs.

Bryson is always willing to move on to something newer and harder. But his ultimate dream of qualifying for, and competing in, the Paralympics keeps him grounded. Although he's young—and not quite ready—he'll keep his eye on the upcoming Games.

The many squads he plays for—track, basketball and hockey—all have clear objectives. They want to provide disabled athletes the opportunity to train, participate and excel in sports. The hope is to build a pool of athletes who can proudly represent their country. The grandest stage of them all, of course, is the Paralympic Games.

In Bryson's case, part of the plan for getting there is to attend college. But not just any school. Several state universities—like Illinois, Texas and Alabama—have excellent wheelchair sports programs.

Bryson realizes every one of these colleges is quite a distance away from New Jersey. But that's all right. He can't wait to venture out on his own.

The University of Illinois is at the top of Bryson's list. He's familiar with the school and the campus because of the basketball camp he attended there. But the university's Adapted Varsity Athletics Program is the real draw. Illinois has a tradition of excellence in wheelchair sports that is unmatched. Student-athletes receive state-of-the-art, advanced training. In fact, the Fighting Illini coaching staff has more international experience than any other. It makes Illinois a breeding ground for Paralympic athletes.

In addition to playing sports, Bryson hopes to study computers in the future. One day, he'd like to pursue a career in technology. "I want to get a good job," he says. "But it has to be one where I can talk all day long."

Maybe he'll play basketball in the Paralympics. Or participate in track at Illinois. Or work for Google. No matter where he ends up, he'll be a success. That's because Bryson McLeod is not content to sit on the sidelines. He's always right there, smiling as he mixes it up, going full speed ahead.

Bryson is very comfortable using computers. He hopes to one day make them a part of his career.

Full Speed Ahead